IN PRAIS
ACCOUNTANTS

If you want to make more money or make bet... for
you. Superb hints not only into how to find your best numbers gu, ~ run
slicker, bigger and better too. Even the biggest figures wuss will feel accountancy ~. ing a
load of this! Goodwin captures the dread of the new businessman perfectly, then addresses every one of
their fears in turn. Fantastic! The must-have book for any small business.

Elizabeth Ashley of Build Your Own Reality.

I'll be honest - I don't like spreadsheets, tax returns or anything finance related, thankfully I
have a good accountant. My relationship with him has grown over the years and he simply takes a
lot of the stress out of my business. I cannot imagine having a bad accountant-client relationship
but I imagine it being a nightmare. Read Anna's book to help you take the stress out of a big part
of your business. Practical and down to earth, just what's needed in what I and Ken Dodd call 'the
mysterious world of numbers!'

Lee Jackson - Motivational speaker / Powerpoint Surgeon www.leejackson.biz

Anna is a special sort and she certainly does debunk a few myths about accountants. I can hear her
definite explanations in her broad, proud accent throughout this book and that is a reflection of who she
is; authentic, passionate and down to earth.

Michelle Mills-Porter of Ethos Development Limited and author of Phone Genius

Running your business can be both exhilarating and scary in equal measure. Your accountant should
be there for you. In my experience as a business advisor, I have seen what can happen if you do not
seek to get the most out of your accountant. I have also seen the consequences if your accountant fails
to keep in contact with you and support you. Anna Goodwin understands this, and, with her understanding of personality profiles, brings clarity to the importance of this relationship. In this book she
will help you understand what you should expect from your accountant, so you can take control and
maximize the value of that relationship for you and the success of your business.

Ralph Savage of DRS Business Solutions Limited

Anna's book 'Accountants don't Bite' is a must read for people running their own business. I remember the nightmare I had many years ago when trying to find an accountant/book-keeper to support me.
In her book, Anna has managed to dispel all those fears about managing your finances and working with
an accountant. If you're looking for someone to lead you through the accounting process in a non-jargon
way, then this is the book for you. It's also delightfully funny too!

Joy Marsden of JM Training Limited

Anna is the most unaccountantlike accountant I have ever met. I know Anna as my accountant, a women's business network leader and a friend. I'm delighted she has decided to share her thoughts and experiences so that everyone has an opportunity to explore their relationship with their own accountant, why it is or isn't working and if not, what to do about it.

This is a book to entertain and educate you about ways in which you can improve your relationship with your accountant. It's a mix of practical advice, anecdotes and thought-provoking questions, all written in Anna's down-to-earth style.

This is definitely not the usual book that you would expect an accountant to have written. Have a look and see what I mean. I promise you you'll be pleasantly surprised!

Jane Noble Knight, The Pilgrim Mother

Anna's book is very informative and written in a very down-to-earth way which reflects Anna's personality. Good helpful tips in what you should expect from your Accountant. Thank you Anna!

Sheila Mc Mahon, Entertainer, Counsellor and CEO of Mind Management for you

Accountants don't bite! …. is a great book for anybody (like myself) whose eyes glaze over when doing bookwork or speaking to an accountant. Plain, simple, easy to understand and apply information using examples and true life stories of how to get the very best from your accountant. Anna has huge integrity and a desire to help people through the maze of their finances. A great read!

David Hyner, www.davidhyner.com

Anna Goodwin has written a very useful book that will be tremendously helpful to both those who are starting up in business for the first time, and also to those who have been in business for a while already. She explains very clearly what you should expect from an accountant and how they can help you to run and to develop your business. In order to maximise the benefit that you can gain from your accountant, Anna details the many areas that need to be considered when working with an accountant so that the reader can make a more informed choice.

In addition to the useful advice and tips that she presents, Anna also includes some spreadsheet examples that the reader can use, and provides a good explanation of some of the key ratios and performance indicators that will tell a business owner how their business is doing.

I think this book will be of use to anyone who is nervous or unsure of talking to their accountant as it breaks down what your accountant will do and what you should expect.

David Jones of Sally's Nannies Limited

An informative and insightful read. Anna's no nonsense approach and clear direction shows that Accountants really don't bite and you can build a mutually beneficial relationship. A must read for any aspiring finance professional or accounting student as an introduction to establishing yourself in the field and how to undertake your practice.

Laura Riley Level 4 AAT Technician Student

To Heather,

Thanks for recommending me to
your clients. Enjoy the book!

All the best,

Anna

ACCOUNTANTS DON'T BITE!

ACCOUNTANTS DON'T BITE!

IMPROVE YOUR RELATIONSHIP WITH YOUR ACCOUNTANT TO MAXIMISE GROWTH AND PROFITABILITY

ANNA GOODWIN

Accountants Don't Bite!
Improve your relationship with your accountant to maximise growth and profitability

Copyright © 2014 Anna Goodwin

www.annagoodwinaccountancy.co.uk

Copyeditor and Proofreader: Siân-Elin Flint-Freel

Design and typesetting: Tanya Bäck (www.tanyabackdesigns.com)

Cover illustrator: Shirley Harvey (www.barelyrecognisable.com)

First published in 2014 by Anna Goodwin

ISBN: 978-0-9930166-0-8

DEDICATED TO MY GOOD FRIEND
RUTH DOUGLAS
You gave me a perspective on things that will stay with me forever.
Thank you.

CONTENTS

INTRODUCTION

If you always do what you've always done, you'll
always get what you've always gotten
—Anthony Robbins

Over the years, I've been continually surprised about people's attitudes towards accountants; this tends to veer from contempt to fear. No one seems to understand that an accountant is there for their clients and can't operate without them.

In order to dispel the idea that an accountant is a necessary evil, I decided to write this book. I aim to demonstrate how you can have a relationship with your accountant; how you can work together harmoniously. To achieve this, I feel that some advice is needed on what you can expect from an accountant. Also, if you are not getting this level of service, I would urge you to communicate with your accountant and if you don't feel that they will change, then, ultimately, leave and appoint another accountant who is more suited to your needs.

The chapters in this book will cover what you should expect from your accountant. They are:

1. Regular communication

To run a successful business you need to know what's going on with your figures. Your accountant must keep in touch with you by using your preferred method of communication, giving you regular updates and free email and telephone support. The relationship between you and your accountant can always be improved. It's nice to hear from our clients and to be kept informed. It's a two-way thing! This chapter will demonstrate how improved communication will help you and your business.

2. Guidance and straight forward advice

A qualified accountant is likely to have studied for a degree for three to four years and then had a period of two years undertaking a professional qualification. Obviously, they are likely to have more knowledge of accountancy than you! This chapter emphasises that advice should be clear and jargon-free.

3. Clear deadlines

To be able to keep on top of your paperwork and prioritise, you need to know when the accountant requires your information. This chapter will explain that your accountant should give you a set of deadlines so you know what you're aiming for.

4. Take account of your skills

Be aware of your own skill level and be honest with your accountant about your level of understanding. Otherwise, the accountant may end up inadvertently patronising you or overloading you. In my experience, this will vary massively from person to person and needs to be explored to get the best out of the client. This chapter gives specific examples of how this can work in practice.

5. Partnership – 100% on your side

As I have already stated, a good, solid relationship is needed with your accountant. This chapter confirms that this is possible and shows how successful it can be.

6. Use of the accountant's skills and expertise

As I've explained under chapter 4, the accountant needs to know what the client's level of ability is so that they can work well together. Conversely, accountants will have a specific skill set and this chapter shows how the client can gain significantly by tapping into this.

7. Help to take your business to the next level

Most businesses aren't happy staying at the level they are when they are first established; they want to grow. This chapter explains how this growth can take place, for example, by changing status from a sole trader to a limited company or by improving management information.

8. Helping to develop relationships

Over the years of being an accountant, relationships with colleagues and clients have been created and nurtured. This chapter encourages you, too, to network and to make your own contacts to help move your business forward.

I have worked as an accountant in Birmingham, London and France – always helping small businesses. With over 25 years' experience of working with small business owners, I feel qualified to advise on how to get the best out of your accountant.

How did I find myself working in France? Well, I had been working in Birmingham for nine years when I decided I wanted to use my French at work. In 1998 there weren't any opportunities in Birmingham so I had 11 interviews in London and got offered a job at 10 of them and another one in Jersey. I decided to take the job at Moore Stephens, London to work on their French property desk.

In France, I learnt to think on my feet. I was carrying out day audits on behalf of the European Commission so everything needed to run smoothly. I still remember having to control a meeting of 11 French people who all wanted to talk at once! Who would have thought growing up in Walsall I'd find myself doing something like this! When I look at my life, it's all about taking opportunities as they arise!

I would like to say I had a grand plan of working for myself but, in reality, it just happened. I had moved back from London to the West Midlands and was working primarily as an auditor (which I found a bit dull!), so I decided to leave. One of my clients said she would like me to continue with their monthly management accounts. She said, "I can understand Anna." – I knew my local accent would come in useful at some point!

I am, and always have been, very interested in people. Maybe this started because of having such a diverse schooling? My first school was a small, friendly one in Bloxwich. Then we moved to France for a year when I was 5; I still can't eat couscous – too much of a shock for a five year old used to plain English food! Later on, I ended up at a formal, strict school in the UK. I came across lots of different types of people, both children and teachers, and found it interesting how they acted/reacted differently.

I was the only person on my Business Studies degree who read all of the psychology books on the reading list — and I was specialising in finance! This experience and knowledge gave me a special insight into relationships between my clients and myself as an accountant. I find Dominance, Influencing, Steadiness and Conscientious styles (DiSC) – working out how people behave – fascinating. It helps me to get the best out of my clients as I can use the language they need and give them information in the format they require. For example, some people with a dominance style prefer to be given short, clear explanations with no small talk. They don't need you to ask how they are or how their dog is! Conversely, you will have more success with someone who has a Steadiness style if you do!

13

My fascination with people and supporting others has led me to be a keen networker. In February 2011, I was supposed to be speaking at the Cannock Women in Rural Enterprise (WIRE) group but I hadn't heard anything so, in the end, I contacted WIRE headquarters. They told me that the Cannock group didn't have a leader. I thought that was a shame, as I know it used to be an active group, so I said, "I'll do it!" I'd never done anything like it before but thought it was an opportunity for both myself and group members. I recognised that it would be a lot to undertake on my own so my sister, Mary Freeman, helps me with the organisation on the day and Cheryl Turner of Tao Business Solutions covers the social media. It's always good to recognise that we don't have to try and do everything ourselves – we can ask for help!

I'm lucky that we have a great group of business ladies who attend – it's networking with a difference as we have belly dancing, comediennes, cakes, displays as well as good business advice.

As I said, I have always been fascinated with people and that fascination leads me to try to understand why some people succeed in business, whereas others don't. Also, to consider why some people accept poor service from an accountant and others don't.

This book will help to define what you should expect from your accountant and how you can improve your relationship.

My aim in writing this book is for you to go away feeling more in control of the relationship with your accountant. By giving you guidance, you will be able to recognise whether your accountant gives you the support that you require. If not, it is very easy to find an accountant who will suit you better. Enjoy discovering more about what is possible...

CHAPTER 1
REGULAR AND EFFECTIVE COMMUNICATION

*If you want to change your situation, start
changing your thoughts about it now.
– Marie-Claire Carlyle*

Communication is a two-way process – if you feel you can't talk to your accountant, is there something you can do about it? I felt this quote was appropriate to encourage you to look at yourself.

My main motivation for writing this book is to get across that it is ok, and even a very good idea, to communicate with your accountant. For a lot of small business owners, this seems an unusual concept and I frequently hear:
- No, I don't ring my accountant because they tell me off.
- I haven't seen my accountant in ten years.
- I don't understand the answers so there is no point in asking any questions.
- I'm worried about speaking to them just in case they charge me a fortune.

In order to have a successful business, it is essential to know what is going on with your figures. You need to have an accountant who will keep in touch with you. An efficient accountant gives their clients a list of deadlines so that they know when items need to be submitted. I go into more detail about deadlines in chapter 3. A list of deadlines (see Appendices 1A and 1B for examples of lists) helps the business owner to plan so that they can give their information to the accountant in good time. Also, it means that they know in plenty of time when they will need to pay either their Self Assessment tax or Corporation tax.

PREFERRED METHOD OF COMMUNICATION

When I meet new clients I ask them how they want me to keep in touch with them. In some ways, the variety of methods with which we can communicate makes life easier but, in other ways, it can cause problems. For example, it's no good sending regular emails to a client who doesn't check them regularly. I note down whether to send letters or emails, whether to send texts or to telephone and whether to use their landline or mobile. Also, I ensure they know that the easiest way to get hold of me is by email or mobile.

After completing a piece of work, clients are given a list of recommendations to improve the information they provide. This gives them focus so that they can concentrate on improving particular areas. Also, because of the flexible nature of the relationship between an accountant and business owner, it also gives them the opportunity to say, "No it is enough work to provide the information I give already – I don't want to do any more. Could you do that bit for me?"

I send information to clients in a format which is as simple as possible so that they are more likely to understand what the figures mean. I remember one of my previous clients saying, "This is Dave you're talking to and I've no idea what you mean!" I learnt a lesson from that!

Some clients may want to discuss an issue face to face.

Ian Davies of Shoenet2020 came to discuss his next course of action with his business. By discussing it together and looking at any possible pitfalls due to timing, he knew what to do next. He said, "What you've just said has made everything clear."

It is a good idea to ask the clients how they want the information laid out to aid understanding. I have found that it's much more useful to give the client, either monthly, quarterly or annually, a few lines showing:
* Sales,
* Cost of sales,
* Gross profit,

- Overheads,
- Net profit,
- Corporation tax, and
- Profit after Corporation tax for the period.

…than a full set of limited accounts.[1] A lot of the necessary accounting disclosures won't mean anything to the client and can easily overwhelm them.

Jane Noble Knight of **Life Fit Limited** keeps in regular touch with me. Recently, she was deciding on whether to undertake a new business venture and we talked through everything in great detail. It's very useful to be able to brainstorm with an accountant as they are independent and have a good, solid basis of business knowledge and experience. They also understand the possible effects on the business's bottom line.

∽

Jane explains how our relationship works and the regular communication that we have:

I'd been with my previous accountant for a long time and I think it's a bit like being with banks – you don't usually change unless there's some reason to change. We had met at a networking event and I got a feel for you and who you are as a person and so I knew that we had interests in common. I started thinking, "You know, maybe I'm ready for another accountant." Then we met up in more of a business sense where you looked at my finances and made some suggestions.

We agreed terms and then I decided, "Yes, that's right for me!" I'd done my research and I'd decided that, if I was going to change, I wanted to make sure it was for the right reasons, for somebody who I could get on with and ask questions of without feeling stupid and who could be a friend to me as well. I started by looking for an accountant I could actually have a relationship with.

I wasn't cost-driven and I know people can be cost-driven. The problem with that is that it may look as if you've got a bargain but if you haven't reckoned on being charged for phone calls and other extras then it can come as a bit of a shock and can be adding on to your total bill.

---

1 Limited accounts – these include a Director's report, an Accountancy Report, a profit and loss and balance sheet and notes to support these. Don't panic, there is more detail in the glossary!

What was more important was having a relationship, agreeing our terms and feeling that I trusted you and that I knew where I stood. We agreed an amount for my limited company for the year and you said that's what it would be unless it appeared that the work was more, in which case you would let me know or, if it was less, there could be a refund so I was happy to trust you in that regard. As it happened, it was round about the cost of my previous accountant but, as I did have extras with that, you worked out to be more reasonable.

I knew exactly where I was; I paid monthly and I felt I had somebody I could talk to all the time. I feel I can send you an email and say, "What about this?" I can make a phone call. It is to do with being timely myself, also, because I am aware of deadlines and sometimes I know I'm getting up to the deadline and I will send you an email to say, "I'm aware it's coming up and this is where I'm up to." But, also, you will get in touch with me so that I have a bit of forewarning.

Sometimes delays happen but I feel that we are both prepared to send each other reminders and I feel it's definitely developed into a friendship where there might be something which is not necessarily business-related but financially-related where I will ask for your opinion. It really works well for me and I'd recommend it to other people.

∽

It is important to remember that the relationship between you and your accountant, like any relationship, can always be improved. It is always good to hear from clients and to be kept informed. It's a two-way relationship, so don't be afraid to get in touch.

CHAPTER 2
JARGON-FREE
ADVICE

One of the 43 Mistakes that Businesses Make:
Not taking good advice.
Getting advice in business isn't hard but getting good advice is.
– Duncan Bannatyne

If you have a business query or don't know in which direction to take your business then you need to be able to ask your accountant. Also, most importantly, you need to be able to understand the answer!

As a business owner, you need this guidance and advice both when you first start up in business or take on a new accountant and, also, on an ongoing basis. The relationship with your accountant needs to be such that you're happy to ask questions to help move you forward.

Most accountants will offer a free business review prior to taking on a new client. This gives both the client and the accountant an opportunity to decide if they want to work together. When I meet a potential client, I ask them to bring along examples of how they file and record their income and expenditure. I also suggest that they make a list of questions that they have regarding their business and accounts.

BUSINESS REVIEW

There are many types of questions I have been asked in the past. Of course, some of them are relatively easy to answer, others depend on the particular client and their individual circumstances:

- Should I set up as a sole trader or a director of a limited company?
- How do I set up as a limited company?
- How do I set up as self-employed? Your accountant should be able to show you the relevant forms on the Her Majesty's Revenue & Customs (HMRC) website and, if necessary, help you to complete them.
- What expenses are tax-deductible? Common areas of confusion for clients are whether to claim mileage or a proportion of total motor expenses and the difference between travel & subsistence and entertaining.
- How should I record and file income and expenditure? Simple spreadsheets such as the one in Appendix 2 would be ideal for recording income and expenditure.
- Do I need to use an accounting package, such as SAGE?
- Do I need to be Value Added Tax (VAT) registered?
- How do I set up a bank account and do you recommend a particular bank?
- How do I withdraw money from a business as a director of a limited company rather than a sole trader?
- How do I set up a PAYE scheme[2] in order to pay myself a salary?
- How do I reimburse myself for any expenditure that I have incurred personally? There is a simple spreadsheet I keep for recording this expenditure in Appendix 3.
- Are there any local networking events that you would recommend for my business?

If I can recommend any particular suppliers, banks, services or networks that they require, then I do.

∽

---

2 PAYE Scheme – This is set up to enable an employer to deduct income tax and national insurance from an employee's wages before paying them to the employee. The amounts deducted, along with the national insurance employers due by the company, are then paid to HMRC.

Jayne Differ's experience of looking for an accountant:

Prior to our meeting, I had done some research online to see what kind of information I'd need to know and there are quite a lot of comprehensive pages out there that will tell you what you need to know. Some of them were saying you don't need an accountant, you just do it yourself online, but I didn't feel comfortable doing that. So, I'd got some questions when I came to see you. Within the first few minutes of meeting you, I realised you are very personable, very approachable and friendly and that came across. Accountants have got a bit of an image sometimes haven't they! I know some friends that are self-employed and they've said that their accountants are a bit of a nightmare to deal with so I wasn't quite sure what to expect.

You told me things like what I can claim for, what I can't claim for, when my tax would be payable, how to set up as a small business — you gave me advice because it was all completely new to me. Obviously, this is your area of expertise; you know your business inside out. I suppose I could have gone away and tried to do it myself but I thought if you know that much and that's a little bit you're telling me within an hour or so then you know a lot more and it would just be beneficial to have somebody like you managing my accounts because, in the long run, you're going to save me money.

Maybe you could look at some of these online sites or try and tackle the self-assessment form yourself, as my brother does. I've told him things that you've told me, the things he could claim for and he didn't know about so he's losing out on saving money. Also, a friend of mine who set up about six months ago was quite shocked when I said I'd hired an accountant. She said, "Oh, what have you done that for? I'm going to do mine myself." Yet, I met her a few weeks ago and she said, "Oh, can I have the name of your accountant?" because of the little things I've been telling her that I didn't realise you could claim back or offset and she didn't know that either.

For me, it was making all of that clear — in an understandable way as well. You didn't blind me with jargon which I think some professionals do to look impressive. If I can't understand it, it's no good to me. You put it in layman's terms and, instantly, I thought it's going to be to my benefit to hire you as an accountant. I made quite a lot of notes while talking to you. Also, you gave me connections for websites, business cards and bank accounts. In fact, I did go to the bank you recommended after that and it was really easy to set it up. Little things like that make a difference — I'd got two or three different banks that I'd maybe go to but I thought, "I don't know which one to go with." It's 'fighting blind' a bit sometimes, isn't it? Just nice to have that little bit of guidance.

When I walked away from our meeting I'd got some knowledge of how it worked that I didn't have before. But it's important for me to concentrate on managing my business —

this is where my expertise lies and I don't need to be an expert in accountancy. I just need to know that there is somebody there that I can trust to handle all that for me and I felt that I would get all that from you. Since then, I know that I've emailed you several times with little queries, things that have come up, e.g. dealing with HMRC who have come back with things that I'm not quite sure about, and you are always very helpful and respond.

Once the business has been trading for a while, then things may change and it is important to know that you can ask your accountant for advice as and when you need to as your business evolves.

ONGOING GUIDANCE

The answers to these questions will vary depending on the circumstances of the particular client.

The types of questions you should be able to ask your accountant are:
- When there is a new business expense — is this allowable?
- What is the most tax efficient way of buying a car and should I put it through the business?
- Would it be beneficial to change my status from sole trader to a limited company?
- Should I be VAT registered? If so, can you register me?
- Should I use an accounting package as I have more transactions, debtors and creditors now?
- Can you help me set up a budget?
- When do I pay Corporation Tax?
- What happens if my director's loan is overdrawn?
- Are there any relevant ratios you would recommend I use for my business? (see Chapter 7)

Carl Freeman of FreemanSmith Construction Limited explains how useful it is to work with an accountant who is open and trustworthy:

Without a doubt, the regular meetings are a great help; without them, I would be completely in the dark. With the meetings I get an understanding; I wouldn't say that I under-

stand it at an accountant's level but I can see how it works and the requirements that are necessary within the business. So the meetings have been invaluable.

Sometimes, the accountant is under as much pressure as the person in business but, unless you talk to each other and learn what you are trying to achieve from it, how can you help each other? There are some things that I can't possibly understand without talking to the accountant. In just an hour, we can go through Corporation Tax, dividends and bonuses.

A lot to take in but I know that you have taken some notes, which is good for us. But, every time I come I learn something more and go away and, run a more efficient system.

As you can see, the help and advice given to each client in each situation will vary and it is important for the accountant to have a flexible approach. The accountant is likely to be more knowledgeable than you but should be able to explain clearly and not patronise you.

CHAPTER 3

A GENTLE KICK UP THE BUM

Deadlines get stuff done.
Prioritise, give it a deadline and get stuff done.
– Duncan Bannatyne

This chapter explains the importance of deadlines by looking at both the accountant giving clear deadlines to the client but also the client not needing to chase the accountant to meet these deadlines.

It is important for a client to have clear deadlines so that they can prioritise their work in order to give the relevant information to their accountant at the right time.

The deadlines will depend on the status of a client; whether they are a sole trader or a director of a limited company.

SOLE TRADER

A sole trader only has **one** deadline; 31 JANUARY following the end of the tax year. They will need to give the accountant all of their supporting documentation in plenty of time for the accountant to prepare their tax return by this date. A sole trader tends to have a year end of 31 March or 5 April because it follows the tax year but they can have a year end of any month end. The first year will start from when they commenced trading to their year end. This could be, say, 23/08/13 to 31/03/14 and the tax return would need to be filed by 31/01/15.

There is a comprehensive list of the information you may need to pass over to your accountant in Appendix 1A. I write to each of my sole traders in early March, prior to their year end, so that they can start collating all of their information. The sooner they get this to me, the sooner they will know how much tax they owe or are due to be refunded.

DIRECTOR OF A LIMITED COMPANY

A director of a limited company will have several filing dates which occur in the year.

DETAIL	DEADLINE
Annual accounts	9 months after the year end
Corporation tax return	12 months after the year end
Payment of corporation tax	9 months and one day after the year end
Annual return	Made up date is the anniversary of incorporation and due date is 28 days after made up date
P11Ds [3]	6 July

Sometimes, I find that my company clients are confused as to what their year end is.

TIP - TO FIND OUT YOUR YEAR END

Go to www.companieshouse.gov.uk
Click on **FIND COMPANY INFORMATION**
Enter your Company Name
Click **Search**
Click on your Company
The accounting reference date is your year end

---

3 Form P11D (Expenses and Benefits) is a tax form filed by employers for each director and each employee earning over £8,500 per annum and then sent to HMRC. P11Ds are used to report benefits provided and expense payments that are not put through the payroll which are made to employees by employers.

For the first year of trading, you may have a longer period than a year — for example, an incorporation date of 06/10/13 and a year end of 31 October — your period of accounts will be from 06/10/13 to 31/10/14.

I give my company clients a list of the deadlines that will occur during the year so that they know when I will need the information. I also give them a list (Appendix 1B) of exactly what information I'll need and go through it with them when necessary.

On top of the deadlines enforced by HMRC or Companies House, there can be other deadlines. One of my clients is a charity, The Rape and Sexual Violence Project (RSVP), and they have their Trustees' meeting in mid-September each year. Therefore, even though their annual accounts need to be filed by 31 December of each year, the actual deadline is early September so the accounts can be printed prior to the Trustees' meeting.

I work closely with **Lisa Thompson** of **RSVP**; she is not only in charge of recording all of the accounts but she is also the Chief Executive Officer. By the very nature of her role, it would be impossible if she did not have forewarning of deadlines. The only way it works is for her to know what is coming up and the information I need from her. I set strict deadlines as I know Lisa works more efficiently when she has this restriction.

∾

Lisa Thompson of RSVP talks about deadlines.

I juggle lots of different tasks at RSVP; I gain the funds, look at the strategic direction, manage the finances, I support members of the staff team and I get involved in making decisions about services.

Alongside that, I also juggle setting up the social enterprise, looking after my nieces and nephew one day a week and training for ultra-running but I wouldn't have it any other way, really. Life would be a bit dull if I did just an ordinary nine till five then went home and watched the telly.

There are some deadlines that are set in stone, funding deadlines might be an example, when I have to send off finances to the Charity Commission —— that's an absolute deadline. There are other deadlines that I might set myself or are set internally by other members of staff or trustees. I have tried a new way of working over the last couple of years which is about setting mini goals for each day, which might be reflective of a bigger goal or might be about a small task that I might think, "Well, it would be good to get that done today." When I work in that way, it is a lot better and I'm more able to manage lots of different tasks because I have a focus and it doesn't seem overwhelming.

∽

Lisa explains how it works in practice by setting deadlines:

It helps because I know that you will keep that vision of where we need to be in terms of finances. You'll remind me about deadlines and check-in about how things are going, even before a deadline has arrived; you ask for an update and that's a little reminder to me that you haven't forgotten about that work and gives me a gentle kick up the bum or a push in the right direction. As a charity, if you don't meet the Charity Commission deadline, that is then public information. It gets shown on the Charity Commission website and it reflects badly on your charity.

If there is an absolute deadline, it creates focus and, for me, it creates a level of stress. I use this positively to get me acting on tasks that I need to do to meet that deadline. The deadline doesn't usually kick-in that stress until quite close to the deadline. I have practised doing little and often tasks in order to meet the deadline and doing those early rather then leaving them all until the last minute.

It works if you focus on smaller tasks rather than the big deadline. For example, the annual accounts, the task for now is the first quarter or the task to get to the first quarter is the first month, then that seems manageable and it's the approach that I am trying more. Before you know it, you've done the last quarter and then you've done the whole year.

∽

You are in control when you are aware of exactly what information you need to give your accountant and by when. It means that you can then plan when you are going to sort out the information. The idea is not to have to chase your accountant but, by having a list of deadlines, you are aware of what your accountant should be doing and by when. Therefore, if you haven't been asked for information and it is getting close to the deadline, you should contact your accountant.

CHAPTER 4
DO IT YOUR OWN WAY – BE AUTHENTIC

The magic really happens by taking inspired action even though it's imperfect – build the plane to fly it.
– Lisa Sasevich

I know that, for a lot of us, it's not easy to be ourselves and to not be influenced by how other people want us to behave. Personally, I feel much better when I do what I prefer to do. I choose to work with small to medium sized businesses — not large ones. Being able to choose the clients I work with is a bonus — I don't want to feel I want to ignore the phone call because I can't stand the client!

The choice is yours but I'm convinced you'll find that if you can stand by what feels best for you then things will work out well. The same goes for how you run your business and doing it in a way that feels right for you.

One of the choices faced by my clients is how to keep their books. Often, when potential clients come to me, they feel pressurised into having a software package to record their figures. I ask them, "Why do you think you need to do that?" They usually say, "Because the bank told me to." My reply is always, "That's because the bank wants to make money out of you!"

When choosing how to record information, the aim is to choose the approach that you will be happy with and find the least painful method to keep up to date.

RECORDING INFORMATION MANUALLY

ADVANTAGES	DISADVANTAGES
Cheap	Time-consuming
Easy to complete — anytime, anywhere	Figures have to be transferred to a spread sheet to be useful
Understandable — no new skills to learn	Difficult to edit/amend if a mistake is made

Colin Wild of **Benjamin Wild & Son** is a Gunsmith and Lizzie Southall, his sister, prepares the books and has done so since 1970. She enters all of the income from sales invoices and all her expenses from purchase invoices into her ledgers. She uses these figures to prepare her VAT returns. So, with Lizzie doing all of this, you may ask yourself, where do I come in as the accountant?

Lizzie is very happy completing everything manually, as she has always done. Her work is accurate because she understands that the figures need to be correct as they will be used for both the accounts and VAT returns. She knows what she needs to do and feels confident about it. She has never entered information on to the computer and doesn't want to learn how.

Each quarter, I check her manual figures, agree the VAT return calculations and submit it to HMRC. On a monthly basis, I enter the gross amount being paid onto Real Time Information (RTI)[4] and submit it. At the year-end, I prepare their accounts and submit Colin Wild's self-assessment return. Hence, I take all the computerised elements from them.

---

4 All employers must report PAYE in real time. Each time you pay an employee you must submit details about employee's pay and deductions to HMRC using payroll software.

What does this mean to Colin and Lizzie? Colin knows the amount of tax that he has to pay and by when and Lizzie knows that the wages and VAT returns are correct and have been submitted online. Neither of them has had to spend time learning how to use the computer and, more importantly, they both use their time in the way they want to! I'm sure Lizzie prefers spending time with her grandchildren compared with learning computer skills!

RECORDING INFORMATION ON COMPUTERISED SPREADSHEET

ADVANTAGES	DISADVANTAGES
Relatively cheap as you will probably have no need to buy a specialised software package if you have office software	Mistakes can be made easily
Easy to complete (using my templates)	Formulae can be entered incorrectly
Understandable — no new skills to learn	You may have to learn how to use a computerised spreadsheet
Saves time	Time-consuming if not used to it
Figures can be used to enter into budgets and calculate ratios etc	

Georgina Barre of **Holistic Dyslexia Services** is a Dyslexia Advisor and is very interested in providing accurate figures. She completes monthly Microsoft Excel spreadsheets for her income and expenditure. I use these as a basis for preparing her tax return. As I work through all of the information, I give her recommendations of improvements which can be made. She will then put these into action for future years. Working together in this way means that we both benefit from our relationship.

RECORDING INFORMATION ON AN ACCOUNTANCY PACKAGE

ADVANTAGES	DISADVANTAGES
Up-to-date figures	Can be expensive as you have to buy the software
Easy to enter	Can be time-consuming to learn how to use the package
Can use figures to produce reports automatically	Not always user-friendly and can be incompatible with other packages

Jenny Dixon of **Executive Reach LLP** is an Executive coach who spent a lot of time choosing the accountancy package for her business. She was looking for one that was user-friendly and, as she is focused on attention to detail, she wanted a package that provides her with the reports she needs.

ﾟﾟﾟ

This is what she had to say about working with accounting packages:

I tend to set a day aside in the week to work on the books. I don't need to do it every week; we don't have stock and we don't have employees so that simplifies things significantly. It's mainly day-to-day expenses and the processing of invoices so it's probably two days a month. When there's a VAT return to do, it's probably three.

I've used a software package almost from the start because, when we first set up, we went to Lloyds bank who had a really good programme that came free as part of opening a business account and that got us started.

We have gradually moved to different accounting packages, mainly because the packages we used stopped being administered. We use Quickbooks now. I think it helps that I've worked with money in the public sector before so I've done basic double-entry bookkeeping and I've worked with accountants. I understand what it is I want to do with the terminology and the things that I am looking at on the screen. If I had none of that prior experience, I would have struggled a bit more. Also I am quite a pedantic, organised person and that pays off when you are doing that sort of thing. I don't like stuff all over the place. I couldn't possibly do the 12 envelope style of accounting which I know a lot of businesses do. How some tradesmen, in particular, manage their incomings and outgoings when they are buying materials and putting them on jobs, I just don't know!

∽

Paul Fisher of **Rio Driving School** knows that he is one of the best driving instructors in the country specialising in nervous drivers. He knows his figures are important to growing his business but is aware that it isn't his area of expertise so he delegates all of the bookkeeping and accountancy work to me.

This means he has accurate figures as well as on-tap advice and doesn't have to use his own time to achieve this.

∽

He explains how it works for him:

I have a system in place, thanks to you, which means that on a Friday, early in the morning while I'm having a cup of coffee, it takes me literally ten minutes to record all the details for that week. In fact, ten minutes is probably over-stating it. I was thinking about that — ten minutes, once a week. We're looking at just over eight and a half hours of work a year and I don't know many people who can actually say that their accountancy nightmare is only eight and a half hours.

It's regimented each week and it also means that I'm always up to date. My accountant can always tell me where I am. If I need to make and investment, I can go to you and I can say, "Can we afford to do this given the projections for the year?" I'm always up to date. If there's a spot check by Inland Revenue, I'm always up to date. I haven't got to take a week off to try to get my books back in order. I don't miss those little details, either, because they're always there. I just staple the receipts as I go along and I never miss anything. I remember one year, spending about two days going through a bag of receipts and trying to put them in month order and then trying to separate out the weeks and it was a nightmare. I needed a better way and now I feel a little bit smug because we are approaching the end of the year and I think, 'Yeah, I remember what I was trying to do a couple of years ago and that was horrible.' I'm glad we've worked something out. It's brilliant!

In my job, I want to know the mileage so that's the expenditure. So I can record all my income, all my expenses and then I can also do an electronic payment to myself for my expenses. It's that simple. The only job left to do is to pop down to the bank with the envelope and pay the money in and it's done.

∞

No matter which method you use, you need to realise that your figures need to be accurate; it's no good just relying on your accountant!

CHAPTER 5
A UNITED APPROACH

S**t happens – and it always will. Make sure you have got
the right attitude, the right support system and network
and the right people around you to ensure when bad
things do happen you are able to bounce back quickly.
– Nigel Botterill

An accountant should be interested in your business and want you to succeed. In order to achieve this, the client must trust you. I think that the best way to achieve this is to be available to your client and communicate with them.

An effective accountant does this by:
- Regular communication
- Updates on progress
- Free email and telephone support
- Straight forward advice
- Details of deadlines
- Taking account of a client's abilities and tailoring their approach accordingly

One of my clients, **Darren Murphy**, came to see me, with his wife, Debbie, not knowing which way to turn. His previous accountant had decided that he didn't want him as a client. The problem was that the accountant wouldn't take any of Darren's calls. Consequently he didn't know which tax return had been filed and whether he and his brother had been set up as a partnership or not. I said to them that I would contact the accountant on their behalf and ask him for professional clearance[5] and an update. The letter that came back stated: 'We cannot provide any reasons why we resigned as accountants.' This put doubt into my mind whether I should act as his accountant.

Now Darren was completely stuck — if he went to any other accountant, they would also be dubious about taking him on as a client. I decided to take him on. Now began the process of unravelling what had happened and what needed to be filed. I couldn't, at this point, speak to HMRC as I wasn't set up as an agent. Therefore, I had to brief my client as to the questions they needed to ask. We soon found out that both 10/11 and 11/12 tax returns were outstanding and that they had never been set up as a partnership. I knew that 10/11 was late but I was determined to get the 11/12 tax return filed on time. Working together with the client, being clear on what I needed, we managed to file the tax return on 30/01/13 — a day ahead of schedule!

By taking Darren Murphy on, it meant that they could move forward. Yes they have fines and penalties but they know where they are!

PROCESS TO CHANGE ACCOUNTANTS

If you are not happy with your accountant then change them. Colleagues have said to me over the years, "My accountant is rubbish but it's a hassle to change". It isn't; it's a simple process! Ask to meet up with any prospective accountants so that you can see if you can work together. You need to feel completely at ease with this person so take your time deciding. When you meet them, ask if they meet up with their clients regularly — at least once a year.

∽

5 A professional clearance letter is sent to the existing accountant asking if there are any circumstances of which you should be made aware before deciding to accept the appointment.

Jenny Dixon of Executive Reach LLP explains how the process worked for them:

You've been with us right from the start. When we first started looking for accountants, you weren't the only person that we met with but the thing that hit it off for us was your approachability; we could talk to you and there wasn't such a thing as a stupid question. You have always been very open and accepting of us, which is very supportive.

∽

Once the accountant has the go ahead that you want to take them on, they will contact your existing accountant with a professional clearance letter. This letter gives your existing accountant the opportunity to state if there are any reasons why the new accountant should not act. In the reply to this letter, they will include copies of previous accounts, tax returns etc. You won't need to find them!

Once permission has been granted, your new accountant will ask you for your ID — a copy of your passport or driving licence and a utility bill — and set you up as a client. Also they will get you to complete a 64-8 form, authorising them to act as your agent. By undergoing this relatively straight-forward process, you can have an accountant who you can communicate with. Definitely worth making the effort!

Paul Fisher, who I mentioned in the previous chapter, has been my client since January 2012 when he came to see me as a sole trader. I prepared his tax returns for a couple of years. When he decided to progress his business and go limited, I set him up and guided him through the process of being a director instead of a sole trader.

Paul knows that his time is best spent with his students and using his hypnotherapy expertise to calm anxious students. Therefore, I set up a system whereby he can record his income and expenditure simply and then pass everything on to me to file and record.

∽

Paul explains how beneficial this relationship is to him:

I'm an 'away from' kind of person. I like to move away from trouble. I definitely move away from problems when it comes to bookkeeping. It baffles me and you probably more than pay for your service by the money that you've saved me and the excellent service that you provide by saving me hours and hours and hours of time and frustration.

I save loads of money, loads of time as well (and time is something I don't have much of), being trapped within my own success in my own business. For me, that's probably the most useful; it's having a system which is dead easy to follow and, as long as I do it religiously every week, I'm not going to get into a mess. Having said that, there have been a few weeks when I've just not got around to doing it but it's still pretty simple to catch up.

∽

Lisa Thompson of RSVP explains how having a close working relationship works for them:

It creates that sense that it's a mutual way of working, that you're bothered about that deadline being met, you're interested and you're keen to see whether there's any areas where I'm stuck or may need extra help and so it creates more of a united approach. It feels that you are working together with us to achieve the finances and the end result. It never feels like an 'us and them' approach.

∽

I have met too many people over the years who have not appreciated that they can have a beneficial relationship with their accountant. Know that you can. Work together and use the fact that the accountant is on your side and the effect on your business will be incredible!

CHAPTER 6
LIFE EXPERIENCE

*Unless you try to do something beyond what you
have already mastered, you will never grow.*
— Ralph Waldo Emerson

As we go through our lives we all gain different experiences. It is important to tell your accountant of any business and accounting experience you have which may be relevant to how you are treated. It is always a fine line between overloading a client and patronising them!

As I mentioned in the introduction, when I worked in London I gained valuable experience in using my spoken and written French. If you don't know me, you wouldn't necessarily assume that, as an accountant, I can speak French. Therefore, don't assume in your case either; explain to your accountant if you have any relevant business skills.

When I first take on a client, I tend to explain to them about filing and recording, when necessary. In the case of **Ian Davies of Shoenet2020**, this was not needed as he is organised and already knew how to file well. If I had started explaining the benefits of filing to him, it would have been unnecessary and could have come over as patronising.

I met up with a potential client, **Chris Durkin of CRD Lean Management Limited**. I could tell as soon as I saw his documentation that he was organised and knowledgeable. Prior to our meeting, he had already set up the company, set up a PAYE scheme and registered with HMRC. For a lot of clients, I would have needed to do this for them as they wouldn't know where to start!

Jenny Dixon of Executive Reach LLP is organised and takes great pride in recording everything well and reconciling the bank and VAT accounts. Because of her competence, the recommendations I give her are of more of a technical nature.

Due to the differing levels of skills of my clients, I approach each client differently and with flexibility. There is never one sole trader or one company client who is the same as another.

Here are examples of two sole trader clients and how they have decided to identify the tasks which they want to be completed by their accountant, depending on their business's needs and their experience and knowledge. 'A' shows tasks completed by the accountant and 'ST' shows tasks the client has decided to do themselves.

TASK	SOLE TRADER 1	SOLE TRADER 2
Inputting and submitting wages to HMRC	A	ST
Inputting and submitting VAT returns to HMRC	A	ST
Preparing accounts and submitting the self assessment returns to HMRC	A	A
Preparing a rental account for their properties	N/A	A
Calculating any capital gains	N/A	A

And below are examples of two company director clients and how they have decided to identify the tasks which they want to be completed by their accountant, depending on their business's needs and the experience and knowledge they have themselves or are present in the company. 'A' shows tasks completed by the accountant and 'D' shows tasks the clients have decided to do themselves.

TASK	COMPANY 1	COMPANY 2
Preparing monthly salaries and submitting to HMRC	A	D
Preparing quarterly management accounts and going through them with the directors	A	N/A
Preparing annual accounts and submitting them to Companies House	A	A
Preparing corporation tax returns and submitting them to HMRC	A	A
Preparing the annual return	A	D
Preparing the self assessment return and submitting it to HMRC	A	A

Have a think on which of your tasks could be done by you or someone else in your business, if you want to do them, or by your accountant, should you wish to be concentrating on something else, be it business or pleasure!

It is always the client's decision as to how much or how little they decide to undertake. It may be a case that they can undertake the majority of the tasks but prefer to delegate them so that they can spend their time running their business. It's always up to them – flexibility is the key!

CHAPTER 7

HELP TO TAKE YOUR BUSINESS TO THE NEXT LEVEL

Realistic and Achievable Goals do NOT work,
and set us up for mediocrity....... At best!
– David Hyner

Most business owners aren't happy for their business to stay at the same level from when they are first set up; they want their business to grow.

∽

Lisa Thompson of RSVP explains the changes and developments to her business and how our relationship will develop in the future:

RSVP now is at a crossroads. If we sat on this crossroads, we'd still offer wonderful services but clients would be waiting longer and longer for the counselling service. That wouldn't sit comfortably with myself or the other manager, Angela, and the finances would just more or less stay the same, around about £300,000. We've all decided we can't stay here; we need to move on and we need to grow so the finances need to grow.

We need to double the income so I'm looking at people assisting me with that and utilising their skills to gain more unrestricted funds. Somebody's writing a lottery bid, and somebody else is working on developing relationships with businesses that might be able to assist.

There will be more tasks around finances so you'll be involved in that growth and looking at those extra tasks and, internally, we have to have somebody to assist me with that role.

There's also the social enterprise so that's a new venture and there's lots of different rules around that. It will be a community interest company; it'll be gaining the majority of its income through trading, rather than through grants, which is what we have here at RSVP. I would think that there would be different tax laws and rules which I need to learn and get my head round and, because it would be more trading income, then there'll be different kinds of finances.

We wouldn't have to report to the Charity Commission but we'll have to do more reporting to Companies House so I think you would be involved with that and that learning for us. But, even in relation to purely RSVP doubling it's income, not just relying on grants but trading more, getting more unrestricted funds through sponsored events through legacies and that will change the way the income profile looks so there will be different tasks related to that you could assist with.

∽

Jenny Dixon of Executive Reach LLP explains the benefit of continuing with an accountant through a period of business change if you have a good relationship:

There's plenty of people that ring us up and try and offer us 'Come to me. We'll do it for you. We can do this as well. We'll do that for you. Have you thought about when you close your company down and all that sort of thing.'

I don't need all that now and if we do ever get to that stage we'll work through it with you. I don't particularly want to go and start making a relationship with another professional at this stage and I certainly wouldn't want to work with an accountancy house where I don't see the same accountant every time. You know how we've worked. You know how we've grown. You have a sense about our business in the same way that we do and I appreciate that.

∽

If you have a good relationship with your accountant, there is definitely an advantage in keeping with them through a period of growth or change as they should know your business and the way you operate well. Your accountant should be able to help you to develop as a business and be part of your 'team'.

CHANGING YOUR STATUS

One of the ways businesses grow is for the owner to change their status from being a sole trader to being a director of a limited company. There are several reasons for this which are listed here:
- They may have been advised to do this
- They may want to tender for larger jobs and being limited is frequently a requirement
- They may feel that the business is riskier and like the idea of having limited liability
- They may want to pay themselves dividends

Another reason can be that the business owners can treat their business more seriously. If they haven't previously set up a business bank account, they do so now. Also, there is a definite division between their personal money and the company's money so it is easier to see how the business is doing.

It is relatively straightforward to change status. It is recommended that you try to coincide the date you stop being a sole trader, as near as you can, with the establishment of your new company. If you get all of the information to Companies House by 3.30pm you are likely to have the incorporation certificate by the next day. It is an easy and efficient process. You will need to complete a tax return for the last period you are a sole trader and inform HMRC that you are now a director of a limited company.

It is a good idea to talk to your accountant about whether to become a limited company and how this will change your responsibilities. Getting guidance from your accountant once you have changed status is very useful and means you are less likely to hit pitfalls. In my experience, the area that clients mostly struggle to understand is that the profits and cash belong to the limited company, not them. As a sole trader, the profits can be withdrawn as it is their money. However, for a limited company, the profits can only be withdrawn as a wage or a dividend. Care is needed as clients can find themselves, later on, in a position where they have overdrawn director's accounts. For example, if they've personally put £5,000 into their business, they can withdraw up to this amount. As soon as they are taking more than this out of the business, their director's account becomes overdrawn. This amount is then taxed at 25% at the end of the year, unless it is repaid.

∞

John Darvall of John Darvall Limited shares his experiences of the transition:

I had been self-employed since the middle nineties and then was put in a situation where I had to become a director of a limited company. I expected there would be onerous restrictions on me as a sole trader by being a limited company and what you managed to achieve for me was actually making it incredibly simple. It was a process of identifying what I needed and then coming up with a very simple strategy to commute what was being a sole trader into a limited company. You guided me through the record-keeping process which, ostensibly, is the same as being a sole trader but with a little bit more detail and emphasis on making certain that you've got the information correctly collated and more accurately put down so you know what's coming in and what's coming out.

The biggest thing about it is that you have to treat the company as an individual rather than treating yourself as an individual. You are an individual separate to the company and that's the biggest thing that I struggle with. You guided me through that. Certainly, from my own point of view, I had a few wobbly months just not knowing what I was supposed to be paying or who it was directly attributed to. But it became fairly clear, through your advice, how a limited company should run and what was attributable to that company and then what I could attribute to myself accordingly as a sole trader.

The tax was a bit complicated because you've got PAYE, Corporation Tax and ways of paying yourself, either through PAYE or through dividends. The important thing I learnt was that you can only pay yourself a dividend if you are in profit. If you are not in profit, you've got to pay yourself PAYE which does tend to focus the mind on making certain that you stay in profit and that you keep an eye on your costs a little bit more carefully than perhaps you would do as a sole trader.

I think the biggest advantage for me being a limited company is, with your help and with that management process, I know more now where I am, financially, than I ever did in 18 years of being self-employed. Being a limited company, it makes you focus on knowing what you're supposed to do and having a strategy. There are a lot of advantages being a limited company as opposed to being a sole trader because, having spent almost two decades as a sole trader, you just carry on doing your own thing, hoping it will be ok. As a limited company, you have to do your own thing and you've got to make certain that it is ok.

The conversion was relatively easy and, if you keep on top of your paperwork and don't let it all mount up to the end of the year, it's not too difficult.

∽

Whether you are a sole trader or a director you need to produce, or to have produced, regular financial reports. These need to be at least quarterly but, preferably, monthly in order to be able to make timely and informed decisions. A significant number of directors focus on doing the bare minimum; they send their books and records to the accountant once a year for them to prepare annual accounts and thereby comply with Companies House and HMRC requirements. Once their accounts are complete, they don't even look at them — they just ask where they need to sign. I think they are missing a trick. These annual accounts are your business health check and give the owner a valuable insight into what is working in the business. It is essential to realise that to understand your figures is the key to long-term success.

I am now going to give you further information and examples covering budgets, management accounts and ratio analysis. These are the tools you need to be using to take your business to the next level.

BUDGETS

This is a plan (see Appendix 4 for an example) for twelve months, usually, which estimates the forthcoming income and expenditure of the business. It is a tool to plan and control finances, showing the most efficient way to move forward. It should be prepared annually and then broken down into monthly and quarterly targets. Each month or quarter, a detailed review should be completed to identify the differences between the budgeted and actual figures. If this isn't done then the business owner doesn't know if the annual targets will be met and, therefore, can't put plans into action to remedy the situation.

MANAGEMENT ACCOUNTS

Management accounts can take many different formats but, basically, will include a profit and loss account and a balance sheet.

Profit and loss account

This shows the performance of a business by looking at the sales, cost of sales, gross profit, overheads and net profit figures. It is important to review the actual figures and compare them with forecasted figures and investigate any differences. By looking at these regularly and undertaking this comparison, this will help to keep your business on track.

Balance sheet

This is a snapshot of the current position of your business in terms of what it owns and owes. It shows the assets and liabilities of the business and the net balance is the equity of the shareholders.

KEY PERFORMANCE INDICATORS

Key Performance Indicators (KPIs) or ratios are a measure of how a business is performing and therefore highlights the business objectives and any areas that need attention.

They need to be:
- Most relevant to your business
- Easy to measure
- Appraised regularly

These KPIs can then be compared with your business's objectives to see if set targets are being achieved.

These KPIs don't have to be purely financial. Examples of non-financial indicators are:
- Customer service e.g. dealing with complaints effectively
- Achievement of deadlines
- Deliveries made on time

It is not beneficial for a business owner to look at sales in isolation and assume that because sales are high and increasing that the business is doing well.

Examples of useful KPIs to calculate

Gross profit margin

This expresses the gross profit amount as a percentage of sales.

Gross profit x 100
Sales

- Gross profit is sales income minus cost of goods sold — it is a measure of the efficiency of the business
- Cost of goods sold are costs businesses incur as a direct result of making the sale, e.g. materials, carriage, direct labour

Example
Sales £600,000
Gross profit £240,000

240,000 x 100 = 40% gross profit margin
600,000

A higher gross profit margin would indicate that the business is likely to make a reasonable profit as long as it keeps the remaining costs under control.

Net profit margin

This expresses the net profit as a percentage of sales.

Net profit x 100
Sales

- Net profit is gross profit minus overheads and measures the productivity of the business
- Overheads are costs which are incurred regardless of the level of sales, e.g. rent, insurance, salaries

Example
Sales £600,000
Net profit £90,000

$$\frac{90,000}{600,000} \times 100 = 15\% \text{ net profit margin}$$

It is a useful measure when compared over time and relative to other companies in the same sector.

Working capital ratio

It shows the ability of the business to pay its short-term debts and should be between 1 to 1.5.

Current assets
Current liabilities

- Working capital is current assets minus current liabilities
- Current assets are stock, debtors, cash and bank
- Current liabilities are unpaid suppliers' invoices, accruals, short-term debt, e.g bank overdraft

Example
Current assets £8,000
Current liabilities £6,000

$$\frac{8,000}{6,000} = 1.3:1 \text{ working capital ratio}$$

Growing businesses need a healthy supply of cash — the working capital ratio is a key cash-flow measure. It shows how much is available to build and maintain a business and whether the business can support itself with its current assets despite current liabilities. Businesses with a high working capital ratio can expand and improve their operations.

It is best measured once a quarter to reflect your business performance without being distracted by short term inputs and outputs which will even out across the year.

Debtor days

This shows the number of days, on average, it takes for customers to pay.

Debtors x 365
Sales

- Debtors — money owed to the business by customers

Example
Debtors £20,000
Sales £100,000

20,000 x 365 = 73 debtor days
100,000

Creditor days

This shows the number of days, on average, it takes for a business to pay suppliers.

Creditors x 365
Purchases

- Creditors — money owed to suppliers

Example
Creditors £12,000
Purchases £80,000

12,000 x 365 = 55 creditor days
80,000

I know that there is a lot to take in from this chapter but, undoubtedly, when you are moving your business forward you need to have an even closer relationship with your accountant so that you can work together to a common goal.

CHAPTER 8
DEVELOPING RELATIONSHIPS

Good business isn't just about brilliant deals, it's about mutually beneficial relationships.
— Duncan Bannatyne

By now, you will know how much I believe that it is vital to develop a good working relationship with your accountant. However, for small businesses, it should not stop there. Small businesses thrive on developing relationships with their customers, with their suppliers and with each other. Networking is crucial for businesses as it is an area where we build relationships.

I remember when I started working in London, the partner said to me, "You need to go out and network". I didn't even understand what the word meant and it was more complicated as I was networking in French! The next day, the partner would be all ears to find out how it had gone and my only comment would be, "The wine was excellent!" I went to a Dale Carnegie[6] networking workshop and found out what networking was about and why it can be useful. Most importantly, I found out 99.9% of people find it intimidating. This made me feel better when I went to my next event — and the fact that it was a champagne tasting event!

---

6 Dale Carnegie is the author of How to Win Friends and Influence People — for details of courses see www.dalecarnegie.co.uk

Compare this to the fact that I now run a very successful networking group in Can-nock- Women in Rural Enterprise (WiRE). I am lucky to have such a strong core group of businesswomen who understand the power of networking.

I've heard people say that if they attend a networking group and don't get any business then they don't go again. They obviously don't understand!

To be an effective networker you should:
- Tell people what you do
- Ask people what type of business you're interested in working with
- Help others with what/ who they are looking for
- Grow your business
- Meet up with like-minded people
- Gain support
- Build relationships with potential clients, suppliers and friends
- HAVE FUN!

A lot to achieve. How do you do it effectively?
- Be yourself
- Keep any introduction short and to the point — don't drone on!
- Help others and offer solutions
- Have one-to-ones so you can learn about others
- Display your products so people can see, touch and try them
- Speak if the opportunity arises and you want to do it. Don't do it because you feel you should. I've seen too many people shaking like a leaf — it's not worth it! There'll be other ways you can excel with networking
- Ask for help

WHAT SUCCESSES HAVE EFFECTIVE NETWORKERS HAD?

Sheila McMahon of Mind Management for You

Through networking, I was recommended to be the entertainment for a 10th Business Networking International (BNI) Anniversary. This is a group that meet in Nuneaton. They have a great sense of fun. The event's organiser wanted to get one over on the group so what he did was invite me to one of their breakfast meetings with my 'Counsellor hat' on, promoting my counselling services. While I was there, I took loads of notes about the participants so I had loads of info to use to come back as the comedian! At the Anniversary, and before the entertainment was announced, I was sitting in the audience, still finding out very interesting and embarrassing stories so when people realised that I was the comedian it was a shock! This added to the night. They took it all in great spirits and we all had a wonderful night!

Other networking successes have resulted in me having the privilege to perform and raise money for organisations including Caudwell Children and The Pathways Project.

I continue to meet wonderful and like-minded people through networking. Networking gives me opportunities and for that I am grateful.

∽

Shirley Harvey of Barely Recognisable

I can honestly say that it is through networking at WiRE that my life has been transformed in so many ways.

I initially started networking thinking it was about making business contacts to help you with your business and found myself in the wrong networking groups, ones where every business there was just out to get more business and not really interested in what anyone else was offering — and I, too, had that mentality. But then I realised it wasn't working for me and I'd come away feeling rubbish about my business.

I then joined WiRE and, to my delight, found a room full of women who wanted to support each other and share in the joy of each other's businesses and their own.

I had reached a point in my career where I needed a business mentor who could guide me in the feminine, more spiritual aspects of running a business that was authentic to who I was. There at my first WiRE meeting stood my new mentor, Jane Noble Knight, as if the universe had answered my prayers (which of course it had!).

Through working with Jane and joining her Pilgrim Mothers support group, I have found invaluable support and networking with a group of women all passionate about following their dreams in business and being authentic.

I am now living in a different country, have begun a whole new chapter to my business that is both deeply authentic to me and completely in alignment with my soul's purpose. I have continued to work with several of the women from both WiRE and the Pilgrim Mother's group, using their services for my business and receiving their support and friendship for the transitions I have gone through. I have been able to give back too, equally, with payment, or support, or with my own skills as a homoeopath, art work and writing.

The support and companionship I have found through networking has changed my life but it took me a long time to listen to my voice within and realise that it wasn't networking that wasn't working for me before but, actually, that I was networking in ALL the wrong places. Once I found the network place that was right for me and my business, I found my tribe and networking has never been something I've dreaded since.

It has become an immensely joyful, supportive, nurturing and abundant thing to do for me and my business. I recommend to everyone in business that they NEED to network — but not with the aim to gain business. To do it with the aim to share your gifts, love and support with others and that you may find your tribe who share with you their gifts, love and support. So, if networking isn't right for you, it's because you are in the wrong networking group. Go find the one that is right for you, turn up and give.

An example of a good networker

I met **Annie Day** of **Heaven Scent Bliss** at WiRE Stafford many years ago and I am glad to say she regularly attends WiRE Cannock. Her energy and passion for what she does is fantastic and she livens up every meeting she attends. She embodies naturally the points I've listed about successful networking. As soon as the meeting starts, she lists down the attendants as they speak and gives referrals to them if at all possible.

Annie is one of the few therapists I know who is always busy. She explains here how she gets her business:

I know I'm an excellent networker and I would say that word of mouth is often how I get my business so it'll traditionally be women and children and they'll persuade their husband or boyfriend or son to come for treatment. We have got a very good website as well that brings in some business but I would think that the majority of the work I get, I get through networking.

I really love WiRE and just being able to go to a meeting anywhere has been really brilliant, particularly the one that you run at Cannock; it's one of my favourite ones because it's local as well, that's really quite important to me.

But I also do some networking that is mixed groups so it'll be a mixture. Traditionally, there will be more males than females at mixed groups and I think that's probably the reason why 60% of my clients are male because I'm actually there every week or alternate weeks, putting complementary medicine underneath their noses. Talking about the benefits that people have received as a result of having a particular treatment will then encourage men, eventually, to have treatments with me. To be honest, although men aren't usually open to going to a complementary therapy practice or a beauty clinic, they don't seem to mind coming here. I suspect because it's a home environment as well as a business that there's something quite intimate about acts of complementary medicine that I think just suits it and I know that a lot of people that have come to 'Heaven Scent Bliss' have said it's really helped them because it's very clear that this isn't just my business, this is a way of life.

I remember the first day that I ever did networking. Although I'm a teacher, I'm quite a shy person, really, although that might not be apparent sometimes. But I went to the first meeting and I'd been asked to be a substitute for someone and the man next to me said, "Have you got a script?" and I was like "A script? What do you mean a script?" And he said, "Oh, you need a script." All the person had told me was to read out his script and then to give out my business cards. He completely forgot to tell me that I'd got to talk as well. I'd got a whole two minutes to write my script and I can remember standing up, taking a deep breath and, shakily, reading out my first script. When I first started my Master's degree, four years later, I was actually asked to stand up and talk about why I wanted to do my Master's Degree and because I'd had to get up and strut my stuff every week and talk for a minute on 'Heaven Scent Bliss', I can remember I just stood up and started talking straight away, very confidently. But, eventually you do feel confident so it's been extraordinarily beneficial in me gaining more clients but also making me much more confident in that way that I would describe 'Heaven Scent Bliss'.

I asked Annie what is the biggest success she has had from networking.

I would think my current trip to Turkey.

I met a lady called Deborah Goldstone many moons ago and we've always kept in touch. She's been on my courses, I've been on hers. We do energy swaps at least four or five times a year. I've been doing the Havening technique, which is an NLP cutting-edge tool for really locking in affirmations. I'd been doing them for three days when she phoned me up and asked me would I like to come to Turkey and it would be first class flight from Manchester airport to Turkey. I would be talking about sexual and spiritual healing, which is what my degree's in, and it would be five star accommodation. It's such a massive honour to be invited to talk at it because it is the World Symposium on complementary medicine so that was extraordinary that I've been invited to do that.

Networking is a skill, but we can acquire it and develop it and it isn't a case of having to join a group and pay a fortune in membership to be successful. I've seen too many start-ups, in their first year of trading, spend thousands on networking as they feel this is what they should do. The problem is a lot of them don't get to their second year!

WHAT HAS NETWORKING DONE FOR ME?

From my hesitant start in London, I now love networking and going to different groups. I enjoy meeting people and having one-to-ones with them. From networking, I have found clients, suppliers and good friends, not to forget all the cards and presents I've bought from the stallholders, so it's a win-win situation. I like the way each event is different; you don't know who you will meet.

To conclude, if you're worried about networking then find a supportive group — like WiRE — and contact the leader before you go or see if you can go with one of the regular attendees. The good thing about networking is that, however confident people seem, they will have felt overwhelmed at some point — like me in London!

Enjoy it and make networking work for you!

CONCLUSION

I hope you've enjoyed my book and now it's your opportunity to have a good, long think about your relationship with your accountant. Could it be improved?

Do you have regular communication and know what's going on with your figures?

Do you understand the advice you're given?

Do you know when you need to give information to your accountant and when you need to pay your tax?

Are you aware of the skills that you have? Have the courage to admit that there are gaps in your knowledge and that there may be areas where you need help.

Think about your skills and what you spend your time doing in a working day. Do you enjoy all these tasks? Could some of them be given to someone else to free you up to spend more time on strategic issues or even giving you more time for yourself. Could your accountant help you with some of this?

Would it benefit you to work with an accountant in a very open and honest way to move yourself and your business forward?

Are you doing enough to promote your business through networking?

To have a successful business I believe a key element is to have a strong working relationship with your accountant. You need to be able to trust them implicitly and to believe wholeheartedly that they are on your side. To work in this way with your accountant will get you the results you want and need. Don't settle for less!

I have always worked closely with my clients and aim to empower them so that they know more about their accounts and can do more themselves. With this in mind, I have devised a series of Simple Accountancy Guides so that business owners can do some of the figure work themselves.

BEING RELEASED IN NOVEMBER 2014

Anna's Simple Accounting Guides —
The Quick and Easy Guide to Bank Reconciliations – What goes where and why

Anna's Simple Accounting Guides —
Stress free tax returns – What to give your accountant and when

To keep updated on these books and more, follow me on
www.facebook.com/AnnatheauthorGoodwin

APPENDIX 1A —
THE 14 ITEMS YOUR ACCOUNTANT NEEDS FROM YOU AS A SOLE TRADER.

The 14 items your Accountant needs from you as a Sole Trader...
...it's easy when you know what you're looking for

When an accountant asks for books and records, what do they actually want?

1. **Bank statements for the whole of the tax year for all bank accounts held.**
   - File in number order and check none are missing
   - File them together for the year

2. **Interest earned on bank accounts.**
   - Request from each of your banks — check the correct tax year is received

3. **Credit card statements (if applicable).**
   - File in month order — check none are missing

4. **Self-employed income.**
   - File all invoices for the year together
   - Invoices should be numbered consecutively
   - Keep separate from employed income
   - Paying in books for the year

5. **Self-employed expenses.**
   - Complete each month on computerised spreadsheet — see Appendix 2B
   - Modify to suit your own expenses
   - Check that the total column agrees to each individual column, e.g. Total is £200 —broken down into Bank Charges £20, Travel £80, Training £100
   - Filing — staple all small receipts to A4 sheets of paper and number consecutively — these numbers will be entered into the spreadsheet
   - Filing — all A4 receipts in month order and number consecutively
   - File in a display book

- Cheque books for the year
- List of mileage for the year

6. VAT returns.

- Filed in date order
- Include all supporting calculations

7. P60s — one for each employer.

- Check correct tax year

8. Dividends received.

- File vouchers together for the year in date order — check they cover the correct period

9. Pension Contributions made.

- Details of amounts made during the year and payee details

10. Pension received.

- Pension statement from each pension provider — check it covers the correct tax year

11. Rental income.

- List of amounts received for the whole tax year — each property listed separately
- If agent used then agent statements for the year in month order

12. Rental expenditure.

- List of amounts paid out for the whole tax year — each property listed separately
- Supporting documentation for the whole year, filed in month order and filed as self- employed expenditure above

13. Property disposals.

- Completion statement for each property

14. Home costs — whole year

- List total amounts for water rates, council tax, utilities, house insurance and telephone
- Mortgage statement showing mortgage interest
- Note down the number of rooms in the house, excluding kitchen and bathroom, and the average number of hours used per week

APPENDIX 1B —
THE 14 ITEMS YOUR ACCOUNTANT NEEDS
FROM YOU AS A LIMITED COMPANY

*The 14 items your Accountant needs from
you as a Limited Company...
...it's easy when you know what you're looking for*

When an accountant asks for books and records, what do they actually want?

Business

1. **Bank statements for the whole of the year for all bank accounts held.**
   - File in number order and check none are missing
   - File them together for the year

2. **Credit card statements (if applicable).**
   - File in month order — check none are missing

3. **Income.**
   - File all invoices for the year together
   - Invoices should be numbered consecutively
   - Keep separate from employed income
   - Paying-in books for the year

4. **Expenditure.**
   - Complete each month on a computerised spreadsheet — see Appendix 2B
   - Modify to suit your own expenses
   - Check that the total column agrees to each individual column, e.g. Total is £200 — broken down into Bank Charges £20, Travel £80, Training £100
   - Filing — staple all small receipts to A4 sheets of paper and number consecutively — these numbers will be entered on the spreadsheet
   - Filing — all A4 receipts in month order and number consecutively
   - File in a display book

- Cheque books for the year
- List of mileage for the year

5. VAT returns.

- Filed in date order
- Include all supporting calculations

6. Home costs – whole year.

- List total amounts for water rates, council tax, utilities, house insurance and telephone
- Mortgage statement showing mortgage interest
- Note down the number of rooms in the house, excluding kitchen and bathroom, and the average number of hours used per week

Self-Assessment

7. Interest earned on bank accounts.

- Request from each of your banks — check the correct tax year is received

8. P60s – one for each employer.

- Check correct tax year

9. Dividends received.

- File vouchers together for the tax year in date order — check they cover the correct period

10. Pension Contributions made.

- Details of amounts made during the year and payee details

11. Pension received.

- Pension statement from each pension provider — check it covers the correct tax year

12. Rental income.

- List of amounts received for the whole tax year — each property listed separately
- If agent used then agent statements for the year in month order

13. Rental expenditure.

- List of amounts paid out for the whole tax year — each property listed separately

- Supporting documentation for the whole year, filed in month order and filed as self- employed expenditure above

14. **Property disposals.**

   - Completion statement for each property

APPENDIX 2A — INCOME TEMPLATE

Income			
June			
Invoice no.	Date	Detail	Total
			_____
			0

APPENDIX 2B — EXPENDITURE TEMPLATE

Monthly Expenditure

June

Invoice no.	Date	Detail	Ref	Total	Telephone	Stationery & Postage	PR & Advertising	Professional	Accountancy	Training	Insurance	Repairs	Bank Charges	Sundries
				0										
				0										
				0										
				0										
				0										
				0										
				0										
				0										
				0										
				0	0	0	0	0	0	0	0	0	0	0

Monthly Expenditure

July

Invoice no.	Date	Detail	Ref	Total	Telephone	Stationery & Postage	PR & Advertising	Professional	Accountancy	Training	Insurance	Repairs	Bank Charges	Sundries
				0										
				0										
				0										
				0										
				0										
				0										
				0										
				0										
				0										
				0	0	0	0	0	0	0	0	0	0	0

APPENDIX 3 — REIMBURSEMENT OF PERSONAL EXPENDITURE

Detailed Summary of Expenses

Name:

Date from:

Date to:

Codes: Travel Expenses (T)
Networking (N)
Mileage (M)
Salary (S)
Other costs, stamps, stationery etc.(PPS)

Current slip no.	Date	Code	Description	Amount
1.				
2.				
3.				
4.				
5.				
6.				
7.				
8.				
9.				
10.				

11.				
12.				
13.				
14.				
15.				
16.				
17.				
18.				
19.				
			Total	0.00

Travel expenses (Train, taxi, parking,….)	
Mileage @ 45p per mile	
Subsistence	
Networking	
Other costs e.g. stamps, stationery	
Total	£0.00

APPENDIX 4 —
BUDGET OVER TWELVE MONTHS

12 month period from

Budget	Nov £	Dec £	Jan £	Feb £	Mar £	Apr £	May £	Jun £	Jul £	Aug £	Sep £	Oct £	Total £
Income													0.00
Direct Costs													0.00
Gross Profit	0.00	0.00	0.00	0.00	0.00	0.00	0.00	0.00	0.00	0.00	0.00	0.00	0.00
Gross Profit %													
Overheads													0.00
Travel													0.00
Accommodation													0.00
Resources													0.00
Subsistence													0.00
Telephone - mobile													0.00
Subscriptions													0.00
Insurance													0.00
Memberships													0.00
Training													0.00
Marketing													0.00
Printing, postage & stationery													0.00
Total	0.00	0.00	0.00	0.00	0.00	0.00	0.00	0.00	0.00	0.00	0.00	0.00	0.00
Net Profit	0.00	0.00	0.00	0.00	0.00	0.00	0.00	0.00	0.00	0.00	0.00	0.00	0.00
Net Profit %													
Year to date	0.00	0.00	0.00	0.00	0.00	0.00	0.00	0.00	0.00	0.00	0.00	0.00	0.00

GLOSSARY OF TERMS

Chapter 1 - What are included within limited accounts?

Limited accounts must include:
- A balance sheet which shows the value of everything the company owns or is owed on the last day of the financial year
- A profit and loss account which shows the company's sales, cost of sales and overheads and the profit or loss it has made over the financial year
- Notes to support the profit and loss account and balance sheet
- A director's report
- An accountant's/ auditor's report

Chapter 2 – What is VAT?

VAT is a tax that's charged on most goods and services that VAT-registered businesses provide in the UK.

VAT is charged when a VAT-registered business sells to either another business or to a non-business customer.
- business customers — for example a clothing manufacturer adds VAT to the prices they charge a clothes shop
- non-business customers — members of the public or 'consumers', for example a hairdressing salon includes VAT in the prices they charge members of the public

If you're a VAT-registered business, in most cases you:
- charge VAT on the goods and services you provide
- reclaim the VAT you pay when you buy goods and services for your business

There are three rates of VAT, depending on the goods or services the business provides.
- standard — 20 per cent
- reduced — 5 per cent
- zero — 0 per cent

There are also some goods and services that are:
- exempt from VAT
- outside the UK VAT system altogether

When you must register for VAT

If you're a business and the goods or services you provide count as what's known as 'taxable supplies' you'll have to register for VAT if either:
- your turnover for the previous 12 months has gone over a specific limit — called the 'VAT threshold' (currently £81,000)
- you think your turnover will soon go over this limit

You can choose to register for VAT if you want, even if you don't have to.

ACKNOWLEDGEMENTS

A big thank you to Jane Noble Knight for her support and encouragement to write this book.

Thanks to:

Siân-Elin Flint-Freel for all of her help and time in proofreading and editing. All of the Skype calls were invaluable in helping me to keep motivated and moving forward.

Eleanor Piredda of Making Marketing Sense for all her wonderful ideas and helping me to put them into action.

Shirley Harvey for my wonderful book cover!

Sara Moseley for the fantastic picture.

Tanya Back for her typesetting skills.

Elizabeth Starns for her book writing, Amazon knowledge and general high level of support.

Sarah Wood for keeping me motivated and being there at the end of the week for a few drinks to rejuvenate, ready to start again.

To all my clients and colleagues who gave their time in the interviews.

To all the reviewers for your lovely comments and sparing your time to read this book.

To all my staff who kept the accountancy work flowing.

To friends and family for being supportive.

Last but not least, to Neil Gooding for his ongoing support while I have been engrossed in writing this book.

FURTHER READING

Positive Personality Profiles
Robert A Rohm

Business Nightmares
Rachel Elnaugh

How to Become a Money Magnet
Marie-Claire Carlyle

43 Mistakes Businesses Make ......and How to Avoid Them
Duncan Bannatyne

Botty's Rules
Nigel Botterill

The Live Sassy Formula
Lisa Sasevich

The Book of Riches - The 7 Secrets of Wealth
Gill Fielding

Your Business Rules OK
David Holland

The Inspiring Journeys of Female Entrepreneurs
Jane Noble Knight

Phone Genius
Michelle Mills-Porter

Key Performance Indicators
Bernard Marr

Profit Rocket
Kelly Clifford

Lightning Source UK Ltd.
Milton Keynes UK
UKOW03f1855070814

236558UK00002B/77/P